HOMECOMING

Also by Bo Carpelan from Carcanet

Axel

HOMECOMING
Bo Carpelan

Translated from Finland-Swedish by David McDuff

CARCANET

First published in Great Britain in 1993 by
Carcanet Press Limited
208-212 Corn Exchange Buildings
Manchester M4 3BQ

A CIP catalogue record for this book is
available from the British Library
ISBN 0 85635 996 3

The publisher acknowledges financial assistance
from the Arts Council of Great Britain

Set in 10 pt Joanna by Bryan Williamson, Darwen
Printed and bound in England by SRP Ltd, Exeter

Contents

Departures and homecomings

My first two collections of verse, published in 1946 and 1947, were – as is often the case with young poets – characterized by an intoxication with words and an obscure symbolism, while the 1950s brought with them a greater rigour: I was keenly taken up with a study of the New Criticism, and Wallace Stevens' *Collected Poems* was my constant companion. In an anthology entitled *Forty Years of Finland-Swedish Literature* (1955) I attempted for the first time a summing-up of my endeavours:

> I do not regret my two introductory opuses but consider them artistically less satisfactory, because they perhaps give off too much of the second way of seeing things in the following old maxim to which for various reasons I have become very attached: 'For a man who knows nothing mountains are only mountains, water only water and trees only trees. But when he has studied and learnt a little, mountains are no longer mountains, water no longer water and trees no longer trees. When, however, he has completely understood, mountains are once again mountains, water is water, trees are trees.' This is perhaps an insight at which one sometimes arrives after hard but also enriching work. For me, that work involves an attempt to define and concentrate the material of experience into the greatest possible universality.

I attempted to set out my view of poetry afresh in a preliminary lecture connected with my doctoral dissertation on the great Finland-Swedish modernist Gunnar Björling (1960). Taking as my starting-point the letters of John Keats, I drew a parallel between his 'negative capability' and our modernists' affirmation of 'the involuntary' and 'rest in the unknowable' (Rabbe Enckell). A lyricism that bears the imprint of experience and in its clarity admits of several interpretations characterizes my collection of 1961, *The Cool Day*, in which after six previous books I believed I had attained something approaching a voice of my own, an inner balance. And at the same time an endeavour to achieve as great an exactitude as possible in language and the expression of life: a quotation from Pasternak introduces the collection *73 Poems* of 1966 and states my endeavour:

> Whether the enigma of beyond the grave
> Can be resolved, I do not know.
> Life, like autumn's silence
> Is – precision.

Further condensation and reduction of the linguistic media led to a blind alley, however; I found a way out of it in the memories of a 1930s Helsingfors childhood that are reflected in the collection *The Courtyard* (1969) which – because of its uniform theme and its anchoring in a fixed location – occupies a special place in my output and is very close to me. Throughout the whole collection there is a longing for something that has been lost; 'room' is a key-word that receives a large number of variations. In *The Courtyard* the rooms are mostly inhabited by the poor, the beaten, and the silenced, and I tried to give them a voice that was as concrete and anti-rhetorical as possible. I have tried to pursue this line of 'openness' in my five collections of the 1970s and 1980s, and have attempted to shape my language as lightly and as compactly as possible. The good poem – as I conceive it – aims at what Paul Klee calls a 'creation-parable', it becomes experience-forming, it gives us new eyes, new senses and is in this way forever engaged, both in depth and at long sight. In this openness is concealed the poem's radicalism. No matter in what guise the poet appears – as seer or clown, dreamer or madman, photographer or visionary (where 'or' may well be interchangeable with 'and') – the uncompromising nature of his own aim and direction is what matters.

Years Like Leaves (1989) is my most recent collection of verse and it takes up the themes of the poet's task and his hand-to-hand combat with language, but also has its origin in the primary source of all poetry: childhood. How hard it is to attain that insight in which mountains are once again mountains, water is water, and trees are trees, a clear, precise lyricism, a reflection of human existence, of people's everyday lives and their visions, but also an image of the nature that surrounds them and constitutes them. The poet continues to be constantly open and questioning, with a few words from *Years Like Leaves*:

> A few words sought their way close up to me
> as though they sought protection from something
> that was too difficult to see. I wrote them down.
> This they taught me, the words that came:
> farewells are part of everything that is
> and, when I have dreamt most strongly,
> a homecoming.

BO CARPELAN
January 1991

THE COOL DAY
(1961)

Autumn walk

A man walks through the wood
one day of shifting light.
Encounters few people,
stops, considers the autumn sky.
He is making for the graveyard
and no one is following him.

Silent trees

Will an unknown hand raise the continents
and the song transfix the bird,
the tide abandon the shores
or wash them with a light that will endure?
And I who form the shadow
that my soul casts over things,
will I exist in this poem
or be read by no one?
It is almost midnight,
the trees stand silent.

In the June dawn

Early in the June dawn he rowed
fully dressed, imprisoned by a tie, with rolled-up trousers
over the calm bay, lingered, looked back:
there lay the island, there slept wife and child,
the trees, the winds were resting there,
the first morning breeze came and broke the mirroring water.

Morning, evening

The grass rests cool,
it is morning, evening
in your life.
Near your ways
goes the last day
perhaps hidden in the leafage of the tree
or in those silent cities
where your cry is not heard.

The mute grass

The heart does not accord with its bounds,
nor the poem with reality,
nor reality with God's dream.
What sort of a dialogue is it that transforms you
without you yourself being transformed?
Do not seek in the mute grass,
seek the mute grass.

Circle

There, by the pale tree,
he stood listening to my mother's footsteps.
The mortal is our love and tenderness,
the day that goes miraculous because it never returns.
I who listen to your footsteps in the grass
and you who stand close to me,
perhaps in the grey twilight
they will remember who now dream?

Evening

Fleeting is the dawn, fleeting the day, but the cool evening
brings its twilight, goes like the water of the bay
among the dark trees where they stand, unmoving.
And among waves from a mileswide distance reach us, slowly,
voices, fragments of words that sink through the air –
fleeting, fleeting is our day but the evening lingers in a summer warmth;
cool summer warmth, linger on in the blood that here will darken
under the trees' crowns, under the open, boundlessly open gaze of
    heaven's eye.

Old woman and road

A radiance lay over the ground, where from
we could not see. Everywhere plains, forests
under the blue-lilac sky. Goldlike shimmering
stood the dead reeds by chill water.
By the shore an old woman stooped down with a pail
and walked away through the wood without seeing us.
Then our journey began.
First we learned to follow the woman's footsteps,
her road was lost in the wood.
Then we heard the reeds before the wind reached us.
At last we saw the radiance from the sky,
interpreted that light that comes out of darkness
and smiling dies.

Under the heavenly signs

The darkness thickens and cannot be seen,
your image is reflected in the window.
The wind is beating under the stars
against the invisible in your life
and on the icy road are heard
carriages that were ordered for your death.
If you are moving through your life,
if the wind is beating against your life,
may everything change when you meet
yourself under the heavenly signs
that sway in the darkness?

The mortal

How thick that green that in recall
clothes heavy trees whose cruel shadows
clawlike stretch across the human mind.
How miraculous mortality and grass,

the sunken waves that raise themselves again,
winds that go and then return at end,
birds that flew but once more send
their song new spaces arch and vault.

You break, you die; like coolness your words
brush near the sleeping one who bears your name.
And in upon this time of joy, of fear
you seek your way, into the changes' haven;

a darkness lasts, falls, lifts and falls.
A hair that lifts and falls now covers you;
a moment's space, a depth that speaks
of the lost things that are hidden in you,

of the world like a grass, of the grass's star.
The heavy winds like darkened carriages
draw you past. Thus count your hours away,
least miracles of the miraculous day.

Morning wash

After words about words were said all still remained,
that which was moved by winds, bloodred sank
and again stood in morning stillness before the low eye,
before the hedgehog's snout and the shadows.
With life's mobility and indecision the poem seeks
air currents and stillness, unsuspecting waters,
the dark earth, and creates in its flight
a wholeness. There in my morning rest parts of me
like the stones by the shore.
There the one I love is washing the morning's wash,
cleaner than words, with morning water.
There is my son moving through my life
and all these images that are things and living beings
have already said about the word
what the word cannot say and what the bay says.

Outside the emotion

Outside the emotion, outside the explanations,
outside our greed, our peace and our despair,
the doing-down in print, the wisdom and its teeth:
the nights with voices like candle-flames
and your breathing.

Concealed

No voices speak.
The great heavy worlds like stardust rise,
silent they look past us, inaudible, reflected
in night's springs.
And all the clarity life ought to have
is here concealed,
as if the roads of childhood were closed by the darkness.

Departure

They came to charge you with your life,
the sunlight brushed against one of your hands like a part of your soul,
     slipping away,
in your other, remains of the earth that was you and belonged to the
     darkness.

Your life altered when they spoke, when they divided
body and soul and you were consumed by longing for the one or the
     other;
the sunlight sank and it became night and you said:
'Eli, Eli, lama sabachthani'
as every human being cries in life's silence,
as a bird, a bird you will see, never more.

Between the verses

Between the verses and the life,
the abandoned day and the abandoned paper,
days when you see that love is not merely wind over grass:
this is 'life's day'
and perhaps broken,
and the day lives and is part of its own dark side
turned towards nothing.

Ski journey

I have succeeded my fate,
the snow drifts over the coarse sand,
the ice-channel cannot be seen, nor the years,
the visible cannot be seen, you see yourself,
that void that is you in yourself,
by glimpses, poling itself along
among left-over twigs and poems
where not even the snow is enough for any fire of roses
in your confirmed soul or the dark December.

The cool day

One day in my life I could not see my life,
only skin and sinews, that soil I belong to,
as long as the day's shadows do not rest.
They moved above me, birds or perhaps creatures
from the earth to which I seek my way.
All that was autumn stood not at all alien,
gave as springs give, leaves or shadow,
and a sharpness in the one
who no longer loves but protects the tenderness
took the objects from me, returned them to me in absence.
The leavetaking birds stretched into silence.
So goes a life from our day,
the cool day.

The boy who ran through the rushing water

The boy who ran through the rushing water
has vanished in the mountain. He shouts no more.
You see yourself, perhaps, but cannot hear his voice.
Perhaps you cannot see him in the summer darkness either.
His mother shouts for him.
Now all the flowers stand frail with frost.
It is the winter's snow that falls on the other side of the mountain
and someone who already awaits his image printed in the mountain's
    side.
It is in the unaltered landscape's shadow
where death's birds raise their bright song
calling his voice to mind.

The carriage of memory

The clear road that goes through childhood's forest
is cool as the coolness in your limbs.
Infinitesimal is the weight of the ripening years.
And like a secret movement the carriage of memory glides
past the words and disappears
into the forest that has come to an end and put out its fires.

In the bright night

In the bright eye, in the bright night
the sea sounded like an echo,

of a darkness from the hard breaker
under the shadow of your mountain, my native region;

but your mouth was silent and surely spoke softer
than a wave that broke on the shore

in the bright nights, in the summer nights
when the cool wind returned.

And your heart beat like the leaves of the shore,
gentle and quick in the summer dusk,

faster, then slackening slowly
towards a sleep, as deep and free as death's;

and from the bay came scarcely a murmur,
scarcely a murmur from the cool blood.

The road down from the mountain

The road down from the mountain
to the house, cooling dusk
between the trees' trunks and their voices,
the silent, heavy, wonderfully young.

The years

You have arrived, the morning's boat is here.
The years buzz like bumble-bees in the summer warmth.
Death and flowering – words
for the beetle, lightening in the mown grass,
silent in the darkness.

In timelessness

The walkers disappeared among the shadows,
their voices faded and also you
more distant from yourself,
yet near, as though the words
had lingered among the trees like trees,
or like the image of the trees.
It was in timelessness
where islands rest on water-levels of the hand.

And when the silence lasted you heard
father's and mother's voices;
then a bird followed on,
then their voices became one voice.
It was in the silence when still the forest
adorned life with its leaves
and the day gathered.
Short is the time when we may live.

Premonition

It was the summer's time,
a door open for the night's breeze.
Never had you walked gentler ways
in the morning's dew,
past sleeping shores.
A cloud came,
someone woke up,
you heard the dear voices
and the night's shadow, the last one,
brushed against you.

You who have left us

You who have left us and where the grass
no longer in the evening dimness shows
footsteps that have returned – dark
among the trees stand the metallic flowers

and your eye sees no more that light
that gently in its hand held the earth
you created. A sea-wind
blows out the nightly candles,

the jasmine stands dim at the gate
that never opens.

The great cloud

The great cloud shaped like a wing
descends slowly in front of the sun
like a blood-red leaf from death's tree.
And over the sea's surface glides the evening's bird,
touches the water's surface with its wings,
changing, as though there were no movement
and only the miraculous song, silence.

March snow

Snow under the March sky's flickering light –
over your life rests its dust with the savour of disappearance.
Already for you the murmur of springtimes is past.
You listen, as though a word
had issued from death, from the high expanses
and not been touched by snow.

Winter's day

I write one winter's day,
write off the day and the night, the planets,
go into my house from a harsh sun
and extend those shadows that are swordlike aimed.
It is a day of drifting snow
and with a voice from that which is I
or was.

The bumble-bee in the grass

Louder than the thunderstorm the rester hears
the bumble-bee in the grass that recalls
the small boy, the great cloud
and the water-enveloped years.

They came like birds and were silent,
became fruits and fell
down into that which is not darkness
but a sound in the grass.

And the revolutions of the great worlds,
and the fear of the lesser stars
can be destroyed by nothing, not even the summer
when the children play in the grass.

And you who dreamed of Atlantis,
you who glided over icefields like a bird of rediscovery,
descend into this cool silence,
into this dream, so near

that its hand is a wind that cannot be lost,
a grass that will constantly grow.

The evening

The evening is near the grass,
the bay is moved gently by winds.
The sun sinks its fire
in the cloud.
Clear, without stars, is the sky.

Bitter voice

At some turning, on the way
from the day, through the forest,
in the landscape of the year
an image of the chill sea opened.
No uncertainty lingered like this one,
lay, like a bitter voice in your eye
when already new days had arrived, other voices were heard.

The early morning

The early morning and the early grass,
the roads silent, farms and meadows wide,
the shadows familiar, parts of the light
and we parts of the stillness, the lingering mind.

Through the evening

Through the evening stars shine,
a bird keeps watch.
The trees move in a child's eyes,
the bird keeps watch
until the wind is silent.

Voyage

Voyage over silent waters,
light when the shore darkens,
the islands wander and the clouds.

The inconstant

The autumn's ice, your body out of the shadows,
the inconstant that also is love
and unknown.

Another world

Another world? Another sunlight,
another stillness?

I love that which cannot be chosen.
Two lives did not choose me,

not evening, not break of day.

Simple songs

Simple songs, morning clear –
how many lives and thoughts have set
so that these should rise,
grass, flowers, day, mortality.

Under the same clouds

Shadows mingle with shadows,
the grass with her hair,
dead rests someone, someone who died
under the same clouds.

Boats were setting out their lanterns

It was dark, boats were setting out their lanterns,
fish were being pulled from the water, pale as your skin,
how silently moved boats and men,
the sea closed like your gaze,
a world was effaced.

The day opens

The day opens,
birds hover over the water,
a cloud moves by
and I take up my work again
in order from two words
to win back one.

The horses

The horses stood with bowed necks. When they stretched
he saw the play of their hide in the summer light.
The darkness in their eyes absorbed June's greenness.
He stood and watched them. Suddenly
they caught wind of him, dashed off towards the horizon,
that light space under a pale, distant moon,
as though he had frightened them with his certainty.

At the table your figure

At the table your figure,
over your hand the shadow of the child's head, a fruit,
your gaze through the window fixed to the trees' movements,
the movement mirrored in the knife that cuts the bread,
the use and clarity of things.

The lips

The lips
broken out of the mountain,
an echo
raised to the day.

The army

Reflected in a shattered windowpane
the army passes by and disappears
in the town that closes up, in the wound
that never closes.

Conversations

Conversations built over the years
or traces of your love –
I go into the pinewood's greenness,
with the clarity of a spring the light
streams towards me like a newly-woken memory
of your perished voice –
tranquil, all-enveloped love,
sprung forth from bitter visions,
trees quietly gathered, twisted:
peace you found, Horace, and this mosaic's pattern
that between the greenness of the trees broke on your floor
while their deep shadows settled
over eyelids and the night's vigil.
Friendship, echo,
I see you like a figure of distance
near this fire that is lit by the earth
and like your words in coolness lingers.

Broken pattern

Where have you been, you who were well-known?
– In a darkness,
abstract, crazed.
There walks he who must be transformed
and like dogs
the winds run through his limbs.
You resemble him. From you I can expect nothing
but suffering that is consumed happiness
and near the utmost darkness
the happiness that is consumed suffering
and breaks the pattern.

The flock of birds

The one that has sung grows silent.
Lights go out, clouds
glide over scrubby treetops
and through me
the silence follows the distant, ever more distant
flock of birds.

Tell me

Tell me before you leave me to you
about the tiredness I have felt even at night,
about the world that never slumbers, footsteps
that move towards the same goal –
tell me before you leave me
if anything has been said or unsaid,
you who know everything and do not answer questions
but move above the fields like a heraldic bird.

Speaking rivers are silent

Speaking rivers are silent, the first bright
flakes whirl through the naked days.
In the way that an autumn dies also the harsh
stars' brilliance is silent and our conversations
grow still in a wintry circle where formerly wild the song was sealed.

Long night

Some day when the border between the day before and the day to come
is a scarcely perceptible change of light
and the trees stand like guards outside the window,
some evening in the age of your ripeness a cold wave washes
slowly through you.
You know nothing of that darkness that has settled;
it is God who observes you and turns away, in moonlight,
and the life you live is, compared to this night, short.

People and clouds

With wings the light spreads in the June greenness.
People and clouds cross over the boundaries of beauty,
like the darkness over the evening vault,
like the water over the bursting deeps.

The green tree, the blue sea

The green tree holds above the child
its still arms.

The blue sea is silent, its breathing
mingles with the child's.

It is years ago. You see:
the tree, the sea remain,

the green,
the blue.

The child walks through the grass

The child walks through the grass.
Child, I have sought you
with hands like cotyledons,
with blinding dreams,
through the earth, the tree
I seek you, the sea's tone
and the lifting wave.

The child walks through the grass.
I follow his path
and enclose him in darkness.
Free me! the child calls
through the earth, the tree,
breaks out of life
for a dream, heavier than life
and with its knowledge.

The child walks through the grass.
Out of the summer his voice sounds
to grass and earth
like overflowing rain,
the whole of my country stands clear,
mountains shimmer green,
waters freeze still,
the autumn draws near and sees my eye.

Beside water

Beside water
is perhaps the place where silence was born.
When this childhood broke from memory
broke also the memory of him, Christ,
for this nocturnal world
that is his heart.

Autumn

The swallows that have gathered in the first cold
are silently leaving my landscape.
It is a time that grows more brittle and breaks at my steps,
a gentle autumn ice.
In the morning my fever has left me, I see:
a table, a mountain, a tree.
Thus days go, clear without consolation.

Winter

In the light coolly blooms
the snow,

blue is the shadow that falls
over your eye

where you dream of the mountain's
words,

clear as the sky, followed
by shadows.

The gull

The landscape must be transformed.
the moon be transformed to blood in a black sky
and the leaves on the trees become bronze.
It is your eyes that are tormented,
die and are reborn in that abyss
that divides your world from the world.
You throw yourself over it like one in despair.
Perhaps, when you fall, these your landscapes
are torn from your eye
and you are you and nothing but the gull in the black sky
with the sound of death.

In another Umbria

In another Umbria, amidst drifting smoke
the wind approaches you and you see a clarity,
the light. We rest beneath its vault.
Nothing in life is strange here where you put
your hand over mine on the spring ground,
in another Umbria, in the shadows.
With murmuring water the morning goes
imperceptibly, down the valleys
where other birds sound to the one who is silent,
the sorrow that has grown to calm,
that has held out against the changing of the light.
The day soon tall and the grass tall by the road.

THE COURTYARD
(1969; 1984)

Note

The original edition of 'The Courtyard' (*Gården*) was published in 1969. This edition, which follows the Finnish selection and translation by Tuomas Anhava (1984), contains the original texts with the exception of five poems which have been replaced by nine from the collections 'The Spring' (*Källan*, 1973), 'In the Dark Rooms, in the Light' (*I de mörka rummen, i de ljusa*, 1976) and 'The Day Turns' (*Dagen vänder*, 1983), together with one new poem.

The brown tablecloth hung down over the edge.
I sat under there unseen in the odour of cabbage and warmth.

The sky hung on rusty hooks, the women of the courtyard shrank.
They were the only flowers the summer had.
They carried pails to the back yard where there was no sun.

Father read the newspaper, in the middle drawer of the writing table
    there were
bills, promissory notes, pawn tickets, the rent book, everything in order.

Behind house upon house the sea rocked somewhere like a patch of oil,
could be seen by glimpses if one leaned out of the attic window.
But most clearly I remember the kitchen table, it was seldom cleared.

Life, it was bottomless, it was a matter of being careful,
going out and in with one's skin like a bruise not to be touched.
The sky was completely clear by the beating-balcony.

One had to find money, have the means to live.
One had to have a room, a bed behind the kitchen
and save for a bigger one.

In the courtyard well there was a water as clear as a spring's.

It was hopeless trying to keep the window on the yard side clean.
Perhaps it was an advantage not to see clearly,
roofs and chimneys, indeed, even the sky became friendly
seen from this renunciation. When it rained
the water formed streets of narrow drops, almost silver-coloured.
I considered them closely.
What use I should have for them I did not know.

He used to say: 'a hand's breadth quieter.'
Then he would hold up his hand for inspection. It had travelled the seas.
I saw that it had been used as a sail
and that over the seas there was quiet.

Each word fell like a tone I must forget,
each day, unspoken.
I knew it not, I lived, dreamed,
as before a birthday with presents.

The insides of the earphones were quite hot.
They smelt of shellac.
Inside the blind tuner with its crystal
there was a whisker, aimed.
Sharp voices from the ether spread like iron filings.
Suddenly a clear tone opened on the earth's surface.
It was Mozart, of all people, like a fine smoke
from my cigar-box.

Even if clothes were a problem the food was always good,
even if money was scarce there were the bare necessities,
even if the bookcase at home was meagre there was the library
it was a better school than school
where knees starved and skin felt tight.
Even if it was winter there was a Christmas star,
a candle, a glass on the table, two glasses and my face,
and theirs who now are dead.
They revived to a joy that the everyday withheld.
I was a joy that rose a bit off the carpet.
No staircase has ever since
led to a narrower paradise.

In the winter night I built myself a ship.
It grew as big as the Lusitania, soon filled the whole of my head.
It was like a great white sail,
the prow in the thundering black shipyard.
I launched it in December.
I watched it slide,
something tore it away from me, it slid ever further and further away!
The snow fell in thick wet flakes.
There was a smell of smoke like a farewell, somewhere.

Removal vans gathered the children around them like ambulances.
Everything grew poorer in the merciless light.
The flowerpots like a final greeting at the gravestone of intimacies,
beds, bedclothes, twisted chairs:
all of it crouched under a shroud that came too late.
We were discovered! But we discovered, too:
empty rooms where we once had lived, the stain of grease behind the
    wall-hanging
and the scratched floors, the gas stove rusted to pieces.
Without rooms the soul went crouched, abandoned
to cheap things whose warmth no one saw.
I jolted along in the van, I was a born tenant.

Spring was mostly a biting blast.
In the park where the bottles bloomed when the black snow had melted
     away
old leaves blew.

The boy with hydrocephalus stooped, his whole body stooped,
the days in the shrill courtyard developed a list and his mother
moved away with him –
and his eyes were completely blue and looked without attention
as we played or turned away, as we went past
and the days went past, the walls stood where they stood.

We had nothing to do that Sunday.
The new boy stood suddenly secretive and waved to us.
He had a face like the flat of a hand.
Did we want to see something funny?
If we didn't tell anyone about it?
We jostled up the staircase.
We sneaked into an un-washed-up kitchen.
There was what looked like a hastily interrupted meal.
The boy cautiously drew a curtain aside.
We looked into a room with a woman and a man
who were asleep with pulled-down clothes, with big white skin.
Suddenly the man calmly opened his eyes.
They looked into mine without seeing. Then they changed.

There was a tree in the back yard.
It stood looking anxious most of the time.
On blowy spring days its last year's leaves still rattled along the walls.
Now that I see it perhaps more as a tree
than as the upright-standing broom we took it for
I write in its honour a poem late-born but deeply felt:
> Autumn leaves
> under the bright spring's
> tracery of branches –

Mother spoke of her only a few times.
There was so little to say.
She had lived alone ever since her husband and only son
drowned near Högholm Island Zoo one July night.
She greeted us silently and we greeted her silently back.
She was the only person who hung a Christmas wreath of lingonberry
     twigs on her door.
The third Christmas it hung far into January
and she was not to be seen.
Mother suspected trouble.
They found her, but I was not allowed to see.
Everything, said mother to father, was spick and span
as though she had been expecting a visit.

Sunday has stopped between the storage tanks,
the waste oil gleams in the sun, the harbour is only
an indentation in the sky, filled with the cry of birds –

it hurts the eyes, cuts between the lips
throws gravel in the heart, turns the soles upwards:
goods-waggon goods, fossilized railway sleepers,

and dies, at last, between bridges, in remnants of waves
like a light slap, in passing,
from an icy wind.

The car whirled up dust and skidded
half-hidden in the sun. The fields swelled.
After the rhubarb cream the milk tasted
like bitter metal. No breeze at the windows.

I remember: the wound the barbed wire tore open,
the stretched shadows – and the water dazzles
towards the eyes as then, with imperceptible, hard blows.

Pre-war summer: burning metal,
and the very water tepid and unclear.
Through the suddenly black trees cut a flash of lightning,
quite near. The thunder rattled in the water-pail.

Towards autumn came the beautiful and warming dark.
The lamp under the green shade glowed early.
Father turned a newspaper; from the new neighbours
came a radio's scraping sound, a shouting voice.
But that too was muffled by the faint, stubborn rain.
What was it we were waiting for?
In the memory there still remains
this sense of something having stopped.

Slowly the house expanded out into the darkness with new rooms,
new passages and staircases, a courtyard behind the courtyard,
closed doors where – quiet! – someone shouted complaining,
or was it only imagination, shadows, misapprehension?

Slowly at the same time the house shrank, the walls closed in,
they acquired the skin's colour, colour of tired eyes as they saw
stains spread out across the ceiling, as though someone
were bleeding through the floor, but not a sound was heard.

Slowly we grew older and ran on staircases
that echoed without answer during hot summer days.
The evenings darkened, were filled with windows and lamps.

The smell of gentle rain, of earth, goes sour in the school corridor
where the coats hang like cripples.
Christmas is an endless tunnel
through which the darkness blows as though it wanted to snuff me out.

Sometimes something I lack itself takes shape
and makes life bearable because it does not exist.
I feel I am near the dead
and near the living, all those who are bowed down.

'How he manages with what he has?
                    He has nothing really,
at any rate nothing worth mentioning, a bed, a table,
and food – you know how it is when a solitary man –
my old father wanted to do the same, well, we let him, he just lost weight,
became almost transparent, prematurely yellow –
                    and not that he had to say hello,
even though I always look him straight in the eye:
                    people who avoid looking at one
are perhaps, I dare say, avoiding other things as well!'

'Perhaps he is avoiding living – or is proud.'

'Proud? Who can afford to be?
                    Just as one can't afford to avoid
living. Nor the time to be so high and mighty either.'

51

The elderly man in a room with kitchen alcove
has blackened his wristbands with Indian ink.
He walks with a stick with a silver handle
and tries to keep poverty
within cultivated limits.
He defends himself as though he had
a constant observer.

The master gardener's cottage among burdock leaves
and the harshness that softened towards Saturday,
the wild vine of the concertina, the daughter pregnant,
the moon pale in the shallow ditch.
By the fence the horse, eyes turned away
that saw you listen.

As I walked over the water-soft field
where single cornflowers still remained in the brown stubble
the autumn wind came heavily towards me.
Here many years ago were mostly summer and children.
Really I felt no loss, returned when darkness fell.

No one really knew they were so poor.
Poverty hides.
The children did not answer questions, they had rigid eyes.
They were never there.
They sat in rooms with not much furniture where it was most often dark.
The father probably did nothing, we saw him seldom.
The mother was shy.
They stayed only three months, the coldest time.

All the stars exist in that part of the sky
that is outside the courtyard's roofs.
We must go down to the shore
in order to see their riches.
There are of course sharper windows, streets and voices than these,
and closer.

There was hardly anyone who did not have a secret
from someone else.
It was a condition of life: that it could be lived
in spite of the days.
It was only the elderly who leaned their bodies
wearily against one another, as though they had grazed on the same
      meadow.
We had gardens that climbed out of every crevice.
We hid their fruits in every unseen corner.
We learned caution early,
we learned the plunderer's knack.
One could make even oneself unseen
if one held one's breath.

In the November darkness the water is not water any more,
it moves cold and sluggish as black oil
                              with broken light strewn on top.
It will never be summer again.

Not a single camera was adjusted
the correct distance from her beauty.

Not a single hand was raised
in order to immortalize her face, like a candle.

The distance was too short, the hand was raised,
there was a white light in absolute darkness,

and she fell on the cellar stairs,
switched off as a lamp is switched off when the room is emptied

or filled with one single breath
from the dazzled one

who with hand before face
was taken away.

Those who were keen on flowers had to be patient
until the allotment gardens flowed over: then great
armfuls were carried to dark rooms and placed in pots.
Before that it was mostly lilacs and marigolds
which were no good for anything after they were thrown in the dustbins.
And later there were ordinary meadow flowers
but meadows were rare.

When any grown-up comes down the staircase
we run right away to the side, hurry past without looking up.
When we have reached the top staircase window
we can see the courtyard narrow and lifeless below us.
All who move there are silent.

How the pile of boards came to the courtyard I do not remember.
It smelt fresh, of forest I thought.
There, behind some planks, I discovered a wasps' nest,
hidden, singing.
Alone one evening I took a stick to frighten them,
thrust in, demolished, ran,

ran for my life far into the grown-ups' world,
beat around me, but no one followed.

Next morning I went ever closer by devious means.
But all was still, no secret song could be heard any more
from the ragged paper grey.

The future was seldom mentioned.
Today was enough.
Saturday was best,
father and mother as though they
were children,
and I hear their voices
like the hand at my brow.

There was no one much who read. Mother read.
And I followed, vanished from the world out there.

Far from being unable to tell dream from reality
one learns to see.

One also learns to be prepared for disasters.
It feels like an illness.

What people take for flight is perhaps preparedness.

Self-evident they stood bowed in prayer over their field, on the bedroom
    wall.
There was also the first kiss in marble,
there was the faithful dog – a St Bernard –
that sat through the years in front of a child like an angel.
No one moved, no one took a step out of the frame.
Our clothes rubbed and became too small.
On hot days the yardkeeper sprayed ice-cold water over us,
oh, we screamed like gulls in that fountain.

There was not much to give to the ducks.
Mother turned the breadbin upside down.
The ducks quacked and looked dissatisfied.
The water was black and soon it froze over.
The winter was hard, even the money froze inside the bank.
Saturday evening could only be celebrated every second Saturday.

In all the time I still slept between father and mother
there stood on the table between their beds a caricature of an alarm-clock.
It had a big metal umbrella
from which sparks of terror whirled in the mornings.
Groaning hands fumbled across its face.
One had to throttle it or oneself go mad.
Relentlessly it measured year after year
the heavy time between evening and morning.
When the war came it had a fit and died.

As when one approaches a railway station
one morning as the sun breaks through the mist
and the muddle of cables sets itself in order,
the thunder from the rails lessens, I wait –

As when someone turns his sick face towards me
and I wait, the cold round lamps in the hall
form a pattern that is absent and mute
and the hand is thin, already nearly dead –

and both these feelings mingle, it is endurable
as only the heaviest, loneliest things
one bore as a child and grew with and knew.

Life was given me one morning of snowstorms.
Cloths and bundles were torn from the hands of the poor.
Out to sea there was no horizon.

Gramophones that smelt of foreign cities
blared like sewing-needles Patti and the Charleston.
Roof-metal swelled with damp and burst,

out welled threadbare bonnets, rattan perambulators,
were cut by shaking tramcars,
between the high, steamed-up windows snow gathered.

Life was given me where others shed it from themselves,
bodies that no one saw, only felt in the darkness.
These dead folk: of the living they knew everything,

but of the dead the living knew nothing.

There are inside the gateway
disconnected images – a memory
like a relic,

a dark negative, finally developed
that day I take my leave –

Memory is what in the present
makes the future visible.

Someone has gone out of the room
and left his clothes behind.
What is happening?

Someone cannot manage to close the door.
What was carried out was heavy
as the sofa, the table, the bed.

Now everything has been tidied up, I think.
And the air is fresher
now that the window has been opened.

Now the wall can be painted over,
so that no stains can be seen.
But the dampness hangs there still.

Someone has gone out in the sun,
is hardly visible any more.

Often from the window I saw a man on the third floor right opposite
stand watching the courtyard or the sky,
he stood quite still before the open window,
he stood for a long time, and I wondered what he saw or if we were
        watching each other,
it felt so peculiar and I would have liked
the twilight to have effaced us yet not concealed him.
In order to avoid him I had to lower myself, almost to my knees
and then creep away to sit on my bed with its netted cover
and feel myself seen through.

The bedbugs that had to be smoked out.
The large winter flies that survived or lay between the windows.
Dogs I never remembered having seen in the courtyard,
strange dogs roamed among the rubbish bins, like cats,
breeds that were never recorded.
Pigeons and seagulls sent their shit flying down.
There was no time or money for pets.

'I do not remember it,
only a room where no one sits,
where everyone has left.'

It was only a small trickle out of one nostril.
But the face was so pale that it lay like a stain in the stair-dark.
And the milk bottle had broken.
'Up you get, up you get, wake up, don't carry on like this,'
scolded the yardkeeper, who was pulling at her arms.
He spoke to her, his wife,
as from despair.

I woke up to someone shouting in the courtyard.
I woke up to a smell of gas: everyone lay dead, even me.

I woke up to war having broken out and my clothes burning.
It was completely quiet. Only father snored reassuringly.

I woke up to so many catastrophes.
It was to lie in training for the future.

There was a sparkling in the top row of windows,
the spring was thrown down to us like a quick reflex.

Silently, as out of moonlight, the trees unfurled
their shadowy, suspected leaves somewhere, near the sea.

Five streets, to the right, to the left, four street corners.
Houses where foreign people lived.
It meant running before eight and walking after two or three.
The days smelt of spilt milk in a knapsack.

The girls' legs and plaits flew,
they were tough and ran like sparks.
One day terrible Kauko with his white hair lay on top of
Hanna after a fight and shouted: 'Now you'll have a baby!'
Hanna jeered, wrenched herself free.
I watched her during the days that followed:
the same shrill voice, the same tough legs, no marks.
She had no babies.
It was lies, all of it.

One summer I was at a summer camp.
There we lay in a row on iron beds.
Mother was afraid but that was something we both
had to overcome.
There was a lot of greenery, and school dinners.
There was a railway that passed close by.
We stood and watched the trains go,
now this way, now that.

We fell headlong to cruel ambushes, got up again,
killed in our turn, fired like madmen.
We ran between silences, streets and houses,
or stole breathless out towards the dark,
split up late, came home late and sat under the table-lamp,
and to the question 'Where have you been all this time?'
we answered: 'Nowhere. Why?' or else sat silent.

On the first of September we were able to divide up the children
into those who had been in the country and those who had not.
The ones from the courtyards stood with a brown streak on their
        foreheads.
They looked like country children.

What are these large heads,
narrow brittle joints
darkness that forces its way into
the blood's nerves,
then finds its way through the eyes out towards the light
and makes it poor?

A mist is rising from the stone, the asphalt.
The children are asleep,
no one can see what they are dreaming.

The school-skin went over the stockings and the face,
the desk squeaked discreetly as on shaky foundations.
Suddenly a flock of pigeons rose outside
and our faces turned like screens
in the ice-cold winter morning.

One had to avoid stepping on cracks in the pavement, to spit at cats,
to avoid walking under ladders, to take two stairs at a time
until one's lungs gasped for release from a self-chosen torment.
The kitchen tablecloth had its own demanding pattern.
There were always rules. The exceptions were like the summer's
        swallows,
rare, hurrying cries that were gone again
and the courtyard Sunday quiet.
The rules were there in order to make life more mysterious
than it was.
And one's thoughts moved quiet as a shuttle
weaving the most crooked fabrics
or in colour quite miraculous.

The tired eyes,
the satisfaction at the day's temperature,
the broken ability to fail:
there was in the soul's alcove all the unpaid,
all the pawned,
yet the agility in the hard pressed: many were masters
in the house inside the house that faced the street,
behind the façade of the façades.
I sometimes heard him shouting in his sleep.
The regularity was life's light and salvation
on the shaky surface,
in the shaky house,
in the room with those dark windows,
those light curtains.

It is dark but I try to see
the child running past the lamps
as I ran with long stockings –

It is night and he runs past,
and I shout: Stop! Stop!
But I have already stopped, turned round

without recognizing.

The ones who have been thrown out of their rooms, with their furniture
ashamed around them,

the ones who try to walk completely silently, so that no one
will notice them,

how they attract to them gossip and hate
as though they had seen

something we have not seen, something
we turn away from among ourselves.

Because someone demanded it,
some part of the furniture,
because the twilight was there and a window to open,
upwards, to the sky.
Because others would have been hurt, grieved
had he not gone up the staircase, day after day
with stones from the courtyard.
There was the repetition like a cut
he had to conceal under outstretched wrists.
There were the dreams, shrunken
or great as the hunger in the shaking bed.
Because she was there, and the children.
Because life was there, unavoidable,
Death he had to do without, like a loaf of bread.
There were demands, in the way stone and walls are there.
Because someone in his eyes demanded it.

Come in to where I am. No, you need not be afraid.
If one has lived alone as long as I have one is helpless.
I sit most often and watch you playing in the courtyard.
If I did not have a son who sent me money I don't know.
Perhaps it would make no difference. When most of the time
one has no one to talk to one begins to doubt.
Sit down. You can have a cup of coffee, and you need not
stay long. So it's you. I've watched you grow
since you were small. Here. What I wanted to say
was: if one doesn't have any contacts
one stops living in a way, as though one had been cut off.
One bleeds away, and afterwards one's just left there.
Money helps one to stay alive and yet
it doesn't help. Against that. Am I boring you?
I'm so used to talking to myself
that I can't talk to others any more. Not properly.
Not that the courtyard here really exists for me.
Before I used to read, but now my eyes can't manage.
How old are you now? Ten? Just as well.
Perhaps you won't understand very much of what I'm saying.
Go when you want to. And come back – some time.
If you feel like it. Well, off you go.

To be ill was to feel oneself safe and solitary.
All light from the windows then stood completely still.
Fever drew patterns on the grey wallpaper.

Sounds were kind and smacked so softly on the dry skin.
They came far away from the kitchen and lingered at a distance.
The room grew large as an alien world.

To be ill was to silently close the door on life.
It had to stand and bluster there, outside,
like a drunken neighbour one can ignore.

I never saw my own roof.
It was like others: black swaying chimneys,
bricks like clotted blood that stretched
hard arteries down into the murmuring house.
The wind in the attic slid echoing through frames of steel wire.
The smell of old clothes, of burning – had there been a fire? –
hovered silently around forgotten furniture, bundles of newspapers,
skis, bicycles; or almost completely empty compartments,
prisons for the filtering light.
Below that lived the schoolmaster with the velvet curtains
who could see the sea.
Below that lived another man who could not stand children: red-faced
    as a September moon
he drove every day to his shipping firm
from a fear-stricken home.
Below that lived the Lehtonens with their seven children,
all in business. They were like ants.
Below that we lived, there were four of us,
between eleven and twelve the sun shone into the sitting-room.
Below that there were dark caves that swallow everything alive
and there I stood sometimes as though the whole house
were slowly falling floor by floor on top of me.
It would not have surprised me
had the double floors been full of human hair,
or blood leapt from the snaking water pipes.

The distance to her was like an evening twilight

She looked over her shoulder as she stood bent over the tub
with the water dripping from the half-wrung shirt:
had someone banged a door, was she not alone?
She must have been hearing things.
She suddenly saw her hands move mechanically:
long bony fingers, swollen joints like knots, blotchy red and the
    soapsuds.
She had to sit down on the wooden bench and lean against the
    wash-stand.
It was as though the feeble light had grown yet feebler.

The best days were cloudy quiet days,
no spring unrest, no hard shadows.
I could switch the lamp on early.
And trees in the park stood in twilight mist,
and the old men by the shore between silent boats
fell silent, they also, one by one.
One felt safe, as when a hope has died.

There was when it came to it no doubt
that they would hardly be able to manage in spite of the low rent.
It was not the fact that he drank or that she
picked up strange men when he was away.
What was worse was that they were quite simply foreign, and would
    always be.
Many of the families would not have cared about their way of life
if they had ever come to meet them.
But all that was heard came through closed doors.
She did not even want help when she was beaten.
In the end the landlord gave them notice, after hints.
When they moved we children were kept indoors.
I remember that it snowed the following day
and it was all forgotten.

'Funny that they haven't got him in hospital or whatever it's
called, mental hospital.'
'They probably want to have him near them, he's not unmanageable,
    after all.'
'But to constantly look after him and change him, all the
uncertainty. I wouldn't be able to cope with it.'
'Perhaps the very fact that he is as he is gives them
strength in some way.'
'Yes, well, I don't have any children myself so I can't say
anything.'
'Or perhaps it's just cheaper to have him at home.'
'Well, it wouldn't surprise me if money was on their minds. Yet I
don't think so. They're probably attached to him. They're probably
trying to protect him. But it won't work, they won't be able to.
No one will.'

As with a shame, enticing,
I walked holding mother's hand among cold window-panes,
stood with her in the bank, it smelt of clothes,
father brought housekeeping money,
the day that had been overcast with rain was quickly sunny,

towards night I lay in the darkness with lamps like silver coins
laid on my eyes.

In that house the twilight came like a blanket
over whose edge the sheet gleamed.
The dark courtyard bore a pattern of footprints
as though the voices had lingered there
listening to the fifteen-watt globes of the lamps.
In that house the pigeons sat silent
looking nervously out over roofs where the smoke
twined like ribbons round the moon.

In that house there were footsteps even before people woke up,
there was in their dreams the rattle of buckets
and the low-voiced circle of words around the child
who lay pretending to sleep.
Like the plaster, something was always breaking up
and the violent gusts of wind knocked drunkenly
against the iron edges of the wooden staircase.
In that house there was mortar for all future houses.

How small I was,
I saw someone row out,
alone, one late autumn evening
and followed with my eyes

If a photograph had been preserved it would be brown,
we have frozen there as children, we stand with caps too big for us
perhaps we are shouting or standing still, with twisted smiles,

it is turning brown.

The hour after dinner was completely silent.
It was as though the twilight thickened in the room.
Father's hand shaded his face when he slept.
Things grew older.

The sounds in the courtyard fell slowly as the snow.
Mother sewed through downturned spectacles.
Over my book I saw them with the closeness of silence.
The table-lamp glowed gently.

After exactly an hour he got up.
Life went back to space and time.
When they spoke I felt lonely again.
Everything was light as when the darkness stops.

There, by the edge of the cement wall,
there, along the black soft rim of asphalt
in the lightning clear day
when the smell of burnt film rose,
I leaned forward,
kept my hand still:
a ladybird escaped, crept finally up
like a confused point of joy,
hovering
between shadow and sunlight.
Slowly I presented my hand
as in a dance,
and it reached my fingertip, stopped,
flew suddenly,
and I saw
like a shimmer
the tall beauty
of space.

Down plunged many faceless ones with open mouths,
with powerless arms in wide, crumpled sleeves,

eyes that still saw, mouths that did not speak,
the breathing so heavy and quick, the forehead's sweat,

old people, set aside,
they were thrown down and disappeared.

He must have thought: now it is enough.
He walked towards the door but the door also approached him.
It banged towards him with violence, it stayed locked.
He beat on it so that the staircase shook.
But the door pressed him against the bedroom wall
where the family were asleep.
The door forced him in against the wall, it remained like a bruise
that will not go away.
His head bowed in a corner, his arms at an angle:
he was back in the room.
When he froze the door flew open.
The darkness flooded in.
He could not go out any more.

The silence, it is the silence after those who could not shape in words,
who could not point to the trickle, say: that is my blood,
I am not living, I am dying.
The silence, it is the footsteps that are cut to pieces by doors that close
and those open eyes there,
all that has remained unsaid like an icy chill between those
who once perhaps believed that they…
There is no silence in the silence, no song,
no one listens to the rain.
There is nothing unspoken, there is nothing to speak about,
there is the courtyard, there the old folk, there the sleepers, there are the
     children, there:
even the children are silent, lie in rows.
If they knew that they cannot speak,
would they then speak at last?

I see with eyes too large for my head.
For one sunbeam there are ten falling shadows,
I stand among them, I already know it.

I see those who turn away, they speak with their backs.
I run away but must take everything with me,
will never be free, I already know it.

Children are so small that they can be run over.
Or else they are made to wear pointed hats and given
sticks with stars, made to sing shrilly in chorus
in play-rooms with small chairs and slipping-down stockings
over near Sörnäs Market.
Children are so small that one can pull them by the arm and sew
it on again if things come loose and then stand them in a corner
or make them run around in a courtyard
until one of them falls, or else line them up in rows
and then squeeze them into the primary school's cold Lysol.
In the darkness one can light their eyes
until they glow like pocket torches, or flames!

From the semi-twilight comes someone
who does not belong to the courtyard.
A dirty raincoat, far too big,
a face overshadowed.
He walks like a fear through the gateway,
I stand still.
He comes right past me, stops,
brings his hand near.
I shrink back.

For a moment they approach but most often have no face.
They have peaked caps and hard shadows or thin legs
that lead them out onto the street and further along giddying heights
down towards the sea and the Russian church and the houses where
    only dead people live.
They scatter as seed scatters and are earthed in again between old houses
and emerge gasping for air in the darkness where lonely lanterns
sway and beat against patterned plaster walls with black iron.
There they are clutched by pale girls, tough as their voices are tough,
and have many children by them and move with big mattresses
to smaller rooms where coughing and unemployment live so securely.
On early misty mornings when the spring rises out of the sea
they sit now that the children have cracked out of the nest with long
    still hands
and watch us who play, if they see us, that is, they are hidden
in shabby raincoats that are far too long for them, the stubble of their
    beards is silver-white.
Later they simply disappear.
They lived forty years perhaps in the same warehouse
and walked between streets and in through black gateways
where suddenly no one was.
The days when they were borne away are always in memory
overcast by chimney smoke.

Streets are drawn in different directions.
The sounds carry other sounds away.
When he goes out and shuts the door
he shouts his own name, but silently,
so as not to disturb the neighbours.

Like sitting in a hotel lobby in a provincial town
in a completely foreign country and looking out of the window:
a square without people, the rain falling, the long wait
in the same lifeless room, and thinking: what brought me here?
Why am I miles from home?
What is the point of it, why did I come of my own free will precisely
    here?
Like seeing how inescapable, accidental it is.
And through the rain to see someone solitary walk and disappear,
    pushing a bicycle
and a hankering to follow – talk – no, to sit
in solitude and remember how it used to be, the low windows
facing the courtyard, the rain, no one at home,
any more, ever.

YEARS LIKE LEAVES
(1989)

I

A little before four, in November
when the field's snow turns blue
the woods grow black, the sky grows deep,
life comes to a halt.
A lamp-post among the trees
lights up a shovelled courtyard
that awaits the son's arrival.
Then the day is done,
the hoar frost on the trees
sinks into the darkness, and on fields
where a road stands empty
the wind begins. Palely in the west
the red sun has set.
Each distant lamp reflects
the sense of maybe coming home.
Against a cloudy sky
the trees' bare boughs can scarce be seen.
A little before four, in November
the twilight deepens
like a feeling in its waiting
before anxiety violently cuts.
Five minutes later everything is over.

Someone draws his finger over the table's surface.
There in the mirror inside the heavy wardrobe
visible for a moment are the vague features
of a stranger who held up the threadbare garments
in a darkness full of naphthalene and tobacco.
Years have mouldered. This silent room
stands waiting as though it still
might hear someone calling over his shoulder:
'Everything here is just as it used to be – fantastic!
Wait…' Then, the voice, uncertain and low:
'Someone has been here. Look.' Footsteps moving away,
silence like a cobweb of dreams.
In empty rooms someone has always been,
someone has always come visiting
and changed everything.

The old man asked: 'Are the oaks still there?
There were woods in my day. Are they still there?'
He sat in a mini-house in Monterey,
could no longer remember any Swedish, spoke a few words of Russian.
He sat like his own shadow and saw
with unseeing eyes the cruelly burnt garden –
the sound of the sea was scarcely audible here, gave no coolness.
'They used to dance, the farm-lads, when it was Saturday.'
He cleared his throat, his hands moved uneasily.
'Bagpipes? Or something like that, can't remember,
the trees, them I remember, the mighty oaks, the woods,
it's as though they still could give coolness…'
He looked at me with an almost angry gaze
as though he had guessed the truth. I replied as he wanted:
'They're still there, it's good to rest under them.'
There was a pause. Then, far away now, he said:
'When the wind moves through an oak-wood you remember it, always.'

The light has grown colder, the words fewer.
People rent other rooms, die or survive
but you know nothing of them, not even from hearsay.
They keep away. It may be that on a windy street
you suddenly meet with a smell, a sound
that makes you stop, turn round:
there is only an old woman in a scoop-hat
disappearing into a stairway, an eddy of dust.
Was there something you wanted to say, note down,
something that evades you, incomprehensible signs
on an old wall next to the locked door?
With a key you did not know you had
you go inside. On the stairs you see precisely nothing.
Those who come towards you have already passed,
the woman is gone, what you were about to say
someone else has said; you are too early
or too late, you wait. You are too late.

A fireball, it is said, may be
a bird that has been struck in the crown of the tree
and transformed into a burning sphere
of soot, bones and feathers –
many experts do not believe this at all.

Children who have imagination and read, it is said,
dream about these birds transformed into spheres,
dream about fire, and every sound,
every voice from the kitchen, the rattle of pails
is the lightning's boom of death and fire.

The image of the heaven's stars as glowing spheres
leads the children's thoughts to this:
dead birds eternally hurled towards the deeps,
distant, white as wind and bone,
giddying, frail small bodies.

The wise talk of children's far too lively imagination.
Better to see the stars of space, their beauty
for what it is, and the earth a moon
full of children who cannot sleep,
who lie with open eyes in the silence's fire.

As you step across the border between seen and realized,
between Always and Never Again,
do you perceive that you have given up, the dead
turn away from you as though they recognized you?
Do you believe the garden will never again bear fruit?
That people are swept like dust along streets
where the asphalt sparks with splintered glass?
Is there a mirror in you that repeats
you who turned away, after you said goodbye – is it
a fleeing thief you see, afraid of becoming pocket-moneyless?
You think you have lost your face, sit
in rooms that are foreign and judge existence
according to them: empty rooms. And not even a chestnut tree's light
among shifting tracery of leaves can tell you anything,
or the cries of children, inaccessible, swift as swallows.
The only way out is to direct into the darkness
what belongs to the light. Hopeless has no hope.
You know it. One more spring, dirty and mute.
And yet: to the sight this fragrance of high sky,
to the ear the blackbird's echoing song!
It is as if in spite of everything your prayers had been answered.
There a hint of approaching summer,
somewhere low voices one warm light evening,
there are Once More and the beloved, near.

Here is a field with spring dew,
a view to the south, a cloud
that stops, moves, stops
like a heavy carriage.
The light is changing over roads worn out with travel,
as though they had borne all life's lumber.
Sunlight gleams in the water that has gathered
in the mud's meandering tracks,
but swiftly fades.
You take a few steps towards the dark wall.
The cold wind barely moves the trees.
The darkness falls as though it rose
out of the ground and surrounded you,
leaned over you as once the mother
over her child
submerging it in sleep.

The bumble-bees that increase and diminish their stubborn song
increase and diminish the heat as well – their anger
stops up the window of the sky, divides the ground into sun and shadow.
Sleep on a day like this is confused, in the dream
the room is locked and you will never get the key –
the number is forgotten. The sun moves slowly into clouds.
It is quiet, as in the graveyard of the winds,
where each tapering trunk stands with its back to you, hiding
the meandering path. You did not think
the twilight would fall so quickly?
You thought someone would meet you before the dark?
Years are forgotten – you go trackless and listen no more,
not even to the echo of songs out of black thickets.
When you wake up you look at the window.
Even the violent light there is a sign of darkness.

There came a voice, it said:
because you are silent this is secret,
it remains between us like silence.

You will live on without noticing it,
you will see and experience many things,
rejoice, mourn, go among people

and no one but you will notice it,
there is a wind from the sea in the evening
that has brought you out to the open heights

and you see lights from the city, voices
that carry over the water, see yourself
among those who seek their way down the harbour,

but you are outside the harbour, you hear a voice,
it says: I have been waiting for you,
you are here, there is nothing between us any more,

you are on the move, are free, finally nameless.

'They have no use for me any more.
They turn away when I say:
I speak not of truth, but truth.
It is the speech of the gods that says in me
that the day is loftier than the night,
that light shall prevail.
The light conceals and demands neither name nor honour.
It is the water that rises to the trees of the shore
and unfolds like shadows on the leaves,
those mute lips: it is not the trees that speak
but the breeze that moves through them.
So also does time's breeze move through me,
I must stay awake, so that it leaves me open.
Fire there is, also, torches in the blood
but the true makes muddy: best is clear water.
Thus says Pindar. His goal is mine:
the highest beauty, that is the true.
Beyond that is merely confusion,
not mine but theirs who cast me out
into torments of loneliness.
Thus is the truth preserved unbroken within me.
In deepest darkness the morning is hidden.
To no one is this of advantage except to him
who sees torment's counterbalance in the noble,
that which like a tree turns its crown towards the light.
Invisible am I
and what they see of me is indistinct, undeciphered.
but the song possesses endurance, rises like a bird
for a moment sun-illumined, and this light
remains eternally. I saw it, the song,
saw that it does not return.'

(Hölderlin)

They move under the earth mile after mile,
the meadow rests green, then withers
and leaves moulder, roads
stretch through the darkness,
the roots go so deep, fossilize,
migrate inward towards the towns,
asphalt bends and cracks,
in great heat a shadow burns
against the wall that has struck root –

the roots twist together,
what those who see call crown
is for those who know root,
its sap flows like a dark river
through sun-bright tracery of branches,
roots move up there above
in the wind that sweeps
over the city's roofs and towers,
out towards the sea, the mute deeps.

It is silent and empty in the world.
Good to have not a thought in one's head,
only, beneath closed eyes, quivering of a life,
not to gather it but to lie awake,
remember, forget, see the water flow,
not step in but oneself be the water,
the night and the faint dawn.

It is silent and empty in the world.
What has been said is silent, is empty in the world,
and a winter, snowless, mild as the spring
says that summer, autumn and winter
are sinking away in the silence, and the years
alone are there, without demands and heavy darkness.
He who keeps watch alone dreams alone.

He that showed you up the stairs,
opened the door to the room, then disappeared,
is no longer to be found, they shrug their shoulders,
someone else has booked the room you live in,
you'll have to hide in a cupboard,
if you wait long enough perhaps
the man will come back, nod affirmatively: it's your room,
always has been. He goes, locks the door after him,
you sit motionless on the edge of your bed, from the courtyard
voices are heard, cries, children and grown-ups,
sudden outbursts followed by silence.
Was this it, everything? All this, saying nothing,
abandoned when the time came.
There is a smell of floor-wax and you open the window,
see that it's spring, hear someone coming up the stairs.
The woman in the corridor outside picks up her key
and opens the double lock for the young couple.
'Here I shall live with you to all eternity,' he says.
She laughs: 'Only until the next tenant.'
'You'll have to pay now, cash,' says the woman,
'the last tenant just scarpered, disappeared.'
'We'll take it,' he says, 'we'll take it. A room's a room.'

In the nights the trees murmur like water.
The day beneath your closed eyes is happy and pure.
You move freely, glide as on wind-filled sails
one summer when school is out and you are not sure,

you do not yearn, do not know if it is night or morning,
the skerries out there move slowly on water-currents
and rise up into the light, no one knows about you,
the day blows like dandelion puff, no one knows that you exist

here in this secret clarity, like a light, high cloud.

Then I saw from the window the line of the coast
sink in waves, restlessly driven by the wind
but could not hear the booming behind the moist windows.
People were struggling out along the promenade
with heavy suitcases, as during the war.
Something was happening and was soon unbridled,
carts of lumber creaked mutely past
and the whites of the horses' eyes gleamed with terror.
Then everything was wiped away by the mist of the sound.
When I got out the silence was near.
What I saw was hidden, as when the trees were hidden
by driving smoke in the rising wind
with the tang of seaweed and mud – all as before.
The only thing I could not hear was a living voice,
only the blare of an ambulance driving past.
What had happened was only a memory and therefore lingered.
At night I dreamed that I stood at the outermost end of the pier,
dreamed about black trees being hurled
into the darkness like glowing firewood at an open stove.
Far out to sea in half-waking a foghorn could be heard,
hollow cries from some ship on a counter-course.

(Rungstedlund)

The forest is flying,
haze conceals the trees.
There deepest in the forest
birdsong,
so loud, remote
in these quiet rooms
where the window's curtains
incline over the floor
like bridal trains.
All the windows black,
swiftly sunlit,
all longing dead and new.
It is so silent
where people have died,
the imprints of their hands
are hidden here
in things that have ceased to be.
Come, see me,
like a bird, solitary,
clear and stretched
over the waters, the waters.

(Rungstedlund)

In the midst of a calm, bright feeling
there sometimes comes a bow-stroke of despair
as to the swimmer in summer water an ice-cold current
that makes the gaze alert, the day acute.
In the first movement of Sibelius' Sixth
there is this astonishing, swift glimpse
down into those hidden torments
that are a part of the sea with its mirroring clouds,
and this gaze plumbs the deep,
plumbs the bottom's wreckage and bones, cannot forget
what is deepest hidden in days of June,
quickly expiring, wind-puffs only.

Back one May evening, and the rooms silent.
Low-moving clouds in the twilight
shift the trees further away.
From the table light – not that a light stood there,
but out of the surface itself, out of that nothingness
that is filled by people.
So objects linger and begin to live
when the door opens, the fragrance of spring comes in
and keeps you company a while
and you remember who it was who said:
'I shall return in spring, you will not escape me.'
In that which is seemingly mute
there is a mighty, unheard voice that lives there
like the tree in the forest, in the table, or
the dream in the act, the scent of flowers
before the flowers have bloomed,
before the summer has arrived.

The tree knows in the winter night that the spring is there
hidden in the hard earth, but says nothing.
The wind blows indifferently, bushes stand grey
and as the days lighten it gets more and more difficult,
the concentration, the work, as though darkness were needed
for a necessary calm. Sparrows, restless,
look for fallen seeds by the fence
where mice swiftly creep out and vanish again
as though there were a city under the earth,
crawling, swarming life, and, like a threat
the moth-eaten squirrel's leap up onto the bird-table:
everything threatening in broad daylight, all the dirt visible
under a uniformly grey sky, day after day
and just cold enough so that the snow does not melt –
then a voice says from a well-concealed room:
Be still! There is a language, you know it,
it is in league with days and dreams,
bright fields and mountain slopes the sun has left.
Remember it, wait.

When we went up the stairs we noticed
that there were no windows facing west,
towards forest and sea – we asked the owner:
houses had been pulled down, wall had stood against wall,
that which had been invisible was visible now,
there were views, if we would follow him.
We began this endless upwards climb
on the dark spiral staircase with its worn steps.
We felt ourselves grow older the higher we went,
breathed pantingly – what was this, a fire tower?
This was after all a house to live in.
Right at the top he, whom we did not know
and saw unclearly in the dark we took with us,
opened an iron door. There was a large hall, whitewashed,
window-splays and loopholes through which bays could be seen,
far-stretching forests, in the inlets white sails
and, deep below, trees moving slowly.
It was as if they were trying to show us something, or warn.
We looked westwards. The sun was setting, there was still a glow
on a sheet-metal roof, a childlike churchbell sounded.
He who had led us here was almost black against the light.

He who does not want to be born
yearns when born for the timeless.
Where he is he hides,
what he says is his protection
and the dark clouds that follow him
he has shadowed and given weight
so that the ground from raindrops' fall
may turn green, trees grow, graves
fill with unpenetrated silence.
He who does not want to be born
does not want to die, and lingers in life
as the shadow lingers near the smile,
near the unsuspecting life in the light.

After such long waiting so few words,
so few colours, such lonely sounds.
Objects illumined by harsh days,
as under a grey-vaulted sky
the voice of the sea, the hour dark,
the autumn near.

When he reaches for the glass on the table
there is someone observing him so keenly
that he quickly withdraws back into the shadows
and sees the face of a man who seems familiar
lean forward so that his cheekbones gleam white
while his eyes are hidden in darkness, that darkness he sees
through the window where people are hurrying by.
He feels it as though he had been weighed and rejected
by someone who in his turn quickly withdraws
and speaks to the woman who fleetingly
turns in his direction and then shakes her head.
It feels as though the whole sat-down pub were sinking
as a wire basket sinks beneath the black electric water
among hands and eyes that barely remember
he was there with his anxious heart
and his going-away shirt.

The autumn's silence remains, the haze
between trees of air and gentle fragrance of water,
as once on a spring morning in a southern town.
And the spring is there with birds that raise the sky
with their song, blue-shadowed like the yielding winter twilight.
Summers there are with the stillness of morning, great and lonely,
your hand warm, your gaze open – ; to later
say farewell is to take a step nearer the evening
when conversations grow softer and at last fall silent
and those who are visible on the road are going away, hard
soon to see them as they walk, shadows among shadows.
And the grass that has grown tall and has stopped having colour:
here there was a well-trampled path, eager feet, the children's,
silvery waters that freeze and something uninhabited
in each and everyone's inner town. You try to find your way out of it.
There is a silence outside you in every language,
something is being prepared, it is not you who is doing it,
there is a conversation outside you between hand and eye,
the air is still mild and the autumn's silence a song
in all that is most inward outside you.

There was once a calm and timeless time
when deep dreams' trees that now are dead bled
enclosing in the resin's honey-sheen a flower
or a dark insect, centuries of eager life,
now just a jewel in your hand.
Is there still an echo of lofty music there?
Are within the stone enclosed your dreams
and the murmur of a cool and life-filled tracery of leaves?
A shadow in a stone, soon dead and nameless.

The summer came in May and was soon over.
June came and froze fast with water-pictures by the shore.
Later, after midsummer, the darkness fell more quickly.
Each day the earth was homeless, autumnal.
As although already now he wanted to hide himself away in winter
but was driven by anxiety and longing for the shore.
What he saw there had already been used up.
Clarity existed, but was mostly emptiness.
The winter came.

II

There are still houses with low ceilings,
window-splays where children climb up
and squatting, chin against knees,
watch the wet snow falling
peacefully over dark, narrow courtyards.
There are still rooms that speak of lives,
of cupboards of clean, hereditary linen.
There are quiet kitchens where someone sits
reading with the book propped against the loaf of bread.
The light falls there with the voice of a white blind.
If you shut your eyes you can see
that a morning, however fleeting, awaits
and that its warmth mingles with the warmth in here
and that each flake's fall
is a sign of homecoming.

Did you know, he said
that a hundred years ago
the road to the graveyard
was interrupted by twenty-three gates?
How much time it must have taken to get there,
the dust that settled over everything, and if there was
no gate-boy, the coachman who jumped down
and while the horse snatched grass from the roadside
pulled the gate along the groove in the road
and the horse trotted routinely through
and the one who travelled
saw dark clouds, fields and woods
and everything was perhaps closer then
because of the slow journey.
People died so much younger then than now.
Did they manage to see more than we?
At any rate they visited the graveyard more often,
that can be seen from letters they left behind.
We still have a little way to go.
Then the church will be there, and the dead.

I remember the cottage that was sinking into its wild garden.
When the door to the shop was opened sweet fragrances came out.
A bell tinkled, a woman in a spotted dress
came from a side-room, where a man in braces sat motionless.
I pointed to the jar of red sweets.
I remember that the roots of her hair were black, her hair blond,
that her eyes, peculiarly dead, looked at me
as with a knife she tried to separate all that was stuck
together in the jar. Sweaty, she wiped her forehead.
On the ceiling the fly-paper clamoured, black with flies.
The air in here was motionless, but through the window I saw
birches glittering violently, moving in the wind.
I remember it as though everything had meaning, but what?
I remember that I was lonely, I think, or forgotten.
Perhaps the unimportant is as meaningful as anything important?
I found it hard to breathe, wanted to flee and yet stay.
I fished out a moist banknote, took my paper twist of sweets
and rushed out into life and heard the woman shout something
but could not stay – all was wind and summer
and fields, meadows, fragrant in the July heat.
Barefoot I ran along the hot road
and into the forest's coolness, stopped and saw
the tall, silent trees in that last childhood summer.

The first foreboding came one summer's day.
I am sitting in front of Åbo Castle, standing sideways,
and the photographer – probably Father – must have seen
the sun going behind clouds and the park fading.
Mother closed her eyes, something was being emptied
as out of a too sun-bright bowl, and shadows
being gathered and thrown against the wall
from some nothingness, some threatening ghost.
There is a tree with strangely black leaves.
We sit motionless, do not touch each other.
That summer the heat was full of dust
and the taste of ash filled, I remember, the air.
I sat and fell at the same time, sat, and Father:
'Has the boy got sunstroke?' So cool was Mother's hand
that I could have sunk into this gloom
and vanished forever – this yearning!
We took, I remember, a taxi into town.
Everything was so strange, as though I were saying goodbye,
for the first time, without obvious reason. Now
the day was open, others followed.

They disappeared and left only vague traces.
The life of the streets ran on, doors were closed
and the memories remained sitting there on quiet chairs.
The first disappeared in the war – the young dead.
Others went later – accidents, illness –
hard to remember them all, while the old
still remain as hand, look and step
and the voices, often filled with joy – painfully.
The tracks continue, dark bands across the fields,
everywhere a look, a gesture, uneroded life.
It is the way between the door and nothing that is so short
that you say what you have to say and hardly
manage to finish your sentence before it breaks.
Trees grow patiently and are not concerned about it at all.
Over the mirror in the darkness hangs a bright clean cloth,
you glimpse there someone quickly walking past,
but you are still here, have not moved away.

At what moment did the shadow pass the street,
and we smelt something rotten from the river
where hammer-blows echoed as if space had been riveted
with glowing lightning-bolts to a dark underlayer
where grass forced its way through, grey and rough
as the stubble on the face of a very old man,
the same grass that with eagerness fastens on graves.

At what moment were we warned, and the train braked in
and a uniformed person with a paper face
looked at the boy in plus-fours and plimsolls
as though he were not there – later,
in summer-dark rain, silent flashes like gunfire
and footsteps that passed over our skins – do not say
that we did not know, see, listen.

Someone said: 'It's too late,' and we knew it,
it was too late: trees, fields, people, towns
and the courtyards between tall houses darkened, sank,
disappeared, and we turned a street-corner, were gone.

I won't die, says the child defiantly.
I shan't ever die! It knows what we keep silent about.
What is the hurry? The beds there, the face,
bed-ends of steel, the full wards –
there were they who turned away as peacefully
as though they had said goodbye on some street corner.
Who gave them happiness? Flaming to the brim
was the cup of their days and just flowed over.
Palely landscape, memories drain away. A wind
that suddenly rises, as swiftly dies
makes the day absent and your heart empty.
I won't die, says the child, defiantly,
and the mother pulls it along with her, through the door
and it is silent as though no one would ever again visit
that place where clouds pass low and the twilight is eternal.

Carefully, heavy with her child
mother sits down in the stern of the boat.
Father rows soundlessly out,
lets the oars trail, takes out his fishing rod,
swings the float, lowers it silently
by the edge of the reeds.
Mother looks to the east,
where the sun is rising and gleaming on the trees
that still stand in their happy greenness.
Clouds move under the boat,
the heat rises.
They sit so gently, as though I were already
a part of the world that surrounds them –
I hurry to the shore
but they are already far away in the morning light,
shadows among shifting shadows,
my cries do not reach them.
Perhaps they see someone waving
but they are already far out, disappear
and there are only faint circles,
a scratch on the water,
a barely perceptible ripple towards the shore.

When you died the darkness hung on for weeks
between the sofa and the table, between the wall and the window,
at last in the empty room. The sun shone in
as usual, but no one paid heed to it any more.
The world was emptied of sounds and furniture.
from the cloakroom behind the hall a wind blew out
clothes that had long hung silent and threadbare.
You sat no longer alone, did not need to be
nervous any more, waiting, cut down on cigarettes,
try to remember if you had taken your sleeping pills as usual.
So narrow your face was, so bright your hair.
The whole house that still remains was buried bit by bit,
the life was scraped clean of the fingerprints of decades
on objects and wallpaper, books, on the linoleum.
Your world, a starry sky, sank into the unsubstantial.
Out of the simple, grey fabric shone the fabric of loss,
strong, like tenderness.

Among drawers of buttons, broken syllables,
words on clotheslines, among rows of old shoes
in worn, mothball-smelling cupboards,
among all the rubbish, all the forays on muddy fields
or in ditches, you suddenly find
one lonely hour a great, alien peace.
You remember, there stood a tree with spreading crown
outside the window, it said: 'Trust me,
listen, and if you thirst
the source from which I drink is eternal, my root
goes so deep down in the earth that I have almost forgotten it –
the leaf-trace gleams, the years are filled with song.
What more do you desire? Have you forgotten me who once
sank your childhood in shadow?'

Forty summers ago you set before me
a plate of oatmeal porridge each time
Mother and I visited you. And I ate
with a slight sweat on my forehead. Those were the hot,
sun-drenched summers of the '30's. You and aunt
moved nimbly, and you were the only one
of your generation who was still alive.
Your mouth sunken, your centre-parting white,
your dress I remember always dark.
Everything about you was definite and clear.
Who had said that I liked oatmeal porridge?
It was at any rate something that held us together.
What we know of one another is not always
a basis for the deepest friendship,
but the unspoken, a look, a gesture of the hand.
There was a tenderness in all the harshness –
why did I not ask you about your childhood
in Småland, about all the years with grandfather?
How would I have been able to?
It strikes me now: I am the last
who saw you, remember you. All the others
are dead.

They died in rooms without windows,
she in a linen store at the hospital,
he in an intermediate room
as though they had wanted to get away quickly and not
torment the living too much, be in the way –
outside there were many sounds, but around them
was only a great silence.
The corridors teemed with people,
outside was quiet autumn.
That which was altered then cannot be altered back.
Everything went swiftly, the everyday came and went
as in their lives.
Now the maple stands burning at my window,
waiting for the harsh winter wind
that has perhaps already made a move on distant fields
and will soon sweep the street outside the gate,
that high, dark gate on space.

Swallows flew through the attic windows.
Their quick wings still fill
the fragrance with sun and sawdust. There were
heavy beams, spiralling chimneystacks.
From the small windows we saw the grown-ups
struggling down there like shadows,
saw woods and fields – trees moved violently.
In the lumber of old furniture and cupboards
there were secrets that had no name,
that could not be told and therefore glowed
in the twilight – are still there now
like an eternal anxiety. And at the same time there
is a boundless room of stillness
and swallows' cries, beyond the children,
the thrown-away objects, the cracked beams,
beyond the dead.

I saw the new road several weeks later.
I remember that I followed it into the woods.
It was silent there, as though no one had walked there.
Between the trunks a new-ploughed field was visible.
There must be a farm there, every road
leads somewhere, after all, even a side-road.
Or else perhaps it goes in a circle and comes out
on something familiar. Did I take the new road
in order to meet the old one? Over the earth
there was a scent of bog-myrtle. Suddenly there was
an enclosure, spruce trees, crosses, but no chapel.
There was a silence, as though I had arrived.
I saw into another darkness. Cloud-shadows
moved over the fields,
they came from high above, showed themselves
only to me.

III

To go out of a room,
put out the last lamp,
watch the light return outside,
tell one's emotion:
go, let the door stand open
a little longer, and let the one
who stands by the door
exist for a quiet minute
wholly without I, an eye merely,
wholly without the torment of thoughts,
an eye, cool and without demands
like the floor's light.

Leaves from a dead year are swept by the wind
over last year's grass. Coldly one day in early spring
the sun shines into the room where the eye sits
stiff in its socket gazing back
at what was said and was never said,
all of it mingled together. What I will not attain
stands black between trees still dead
and what I have attained has been scattered,
dust whirls up when a car drives past.
Now is the time of errors, of stiff-frozen flower-shoots
and a tough, hidden life among scrubby bushes.
Boughs are broken by gusting winds, the darkness creaks,
each morning the stubborn grey light sieves
sand over the city's streets and squares
giving dreams gall-sores.
What have you achieved? Someone throws you against a wall
and you become a wall. It is too late
to bribe the future, it sits silently behind the wheel,
it yawns, and you know that you will travel
no more, except from here to there
and back, with the Z bus.
The gale, the atrocious gale
forces tears, and people you know
hurry past in their dark clothes.
You stand and see and do not see, someone sees,
life is swept by the wind,
is no more.

Honey of linden was my beloved's skin.
Never will I forget the time of blossom-fall.
The shadows of the trees and the children's cries
were waves we followed with smiling eyes.
The scent of summer we preserve
in years that have gone, along paths that are overgrown.
Honey of linden is my beloved's skin.

Not everything of course was said.
A window flew open and the wind
moved through the room and settled
in my heart. The silence rang in my ears.
October October with flickering lights
drifted homeless between the walls
and I sat, young, unprepared
and looked down into unknown, dark abysses
where people moved effortlessly on bridges
as though for them nothing had ever happened.
If I sat motionless my mind was hurled
from hope to despair
without shaking a hidden, stubborn conviction
like a firm seed in an unripe fruit
or a candle in a room without windows,
strong, gentle and protecting.

When you cried out I was so far in you
that I saw roads, fields and forests
and hidden in the forest three men hauling a cart
along a white road that lost itself in the darkness;
when I came back you had already been waiting
and turned round and followed the strangers' cry
even though your eye was closed and you open to life.

You stand with your opinion like a landing stage
towards the evening when we both are silent.
There is a safety here like over us the heaven's depths
with constellations you know better than I.
You hear the distant rain and feel the darkness,
see that which is slow to come and say:
let each and all speak in their own breathing,
in their inmost place. Shadow-plays
are play of shadows, nothing else.
You discover a new morning and say: Welcome!

I am in the summer evening
am in the yielding light
the silent space
an eternity's moment
before the day is here
you still by my side
morning and evening twilight
the unspoken we listen to
and share
in our short, clear life

You ask about death. I see it
as a source, another earth,
that which exists here but there is more exact,
clearer, more patient, more full of mystery.

Very possible that once I thought
it was the 'great' simplicity I sought.
Certainly, when the road stretched through narrow
forests, utterly ugly cottages lay thrown out on the fields,
it was beautiful to see how sea and sky
there by the shore reflected each other.
As now from the window I idly consider
some bit of forest with snow-slush under grey clouds,
the slope's bare bushes, forgotten summer gear,
birches and firs, scrubby creepers
I find the 'great' simplicity complicated.
There is far too much that is unseen between trunks,
the shadows of anxiety, and a magpie
flies violently up and is with ugly wingbeats
quickly gone. Icy winter stands at the door.
This hesitancy everywhere, even in the mind:
where then is the simple in the simple?
Where the safe certainty that fields and skies will open
when a forest, a curve in the road suddenly lead
away, past, and are swiftly lost
in their own darkness? And it begins to blow.
But what winds sweep away is often just the rubbish.

Now I want to go into your room
and rest in you
as though the meaning of the days
had been this
and no, no other.

They gathered, this down
these light feathers
the brittle skeleton
the eyes clear, cold
there in the quivering shadows
there in the forest

so that the song rose
lightly, like leaf-thin
honed wood, metal
tenderly hardened by fire
and plunged in water
in its transformations
in its furrows, in sand

out of this invisible room
of air, of cloud
a shaped, hovering wave

So few people,
so many empty chairs
and the sea that indifferently glitters
for no one, waves only
and lulling wind –

so few words
with darkness behind the light
and the completely empty
blue sky

here, under the thorax
after years like leaves
in incurable happiness
and pain

The train returns
to the station
but those one meets
have grown old.
They go their way
as though they were not there.
The luggage stands abandoned
on rusty trolleys.
Under the arches of the hall
fly birds
like smuts
in vapour of white clouds.
A child stands there
with your features
looking up at you
and the closed windows.

Then the teeth gleam in the dark.
Then the breathing passes on
and the attempts of the tormented to speak.
Then the darkness comes among the trees
that are always there, waiting
for the fields' mud and crushed leaves
and for the clouds that drift
like glacial sailboats, past.

Wake up, wake up, the spring is already here
and you have become your own stranger,
see that which grows wither, see in your happiness
a seed, almost a shadow,
and the cold wind that tugs at every newborn leaf.

If one clings like Harold Lloyd
to the clock, the hand always shows
the half-hour. If one lets go one's grip
the terror-stricken actor falls away
and only a naked scream fills the streets.
Turn your gaze away – still you see
the fall, yourself fall slowly:
again you have taken an invisible step nearer the time
when all traffic stops, for a moment,
and then flows unconcernedly onwards.

At last tiredness strikes with a narrow chisel
a crack in the muteness and a few words
trickle out, like resin, moisture and blood
and stain the paper that like a sheet
falls over the body with its open hands.

At last, at last the words trickle out
so weighed down by muteness, so aging,
as though they themselves were bodies, almost forgotten
with the hidden wings dropped
like shields at their sides – at last! at last!

Take your time
take it on your back and feel
how heavy it is.
Put it down gently,
it complains softly,
lull it to rest.
The cool room breathes,
years of flower-scent linger on,
you wait, and one day
timelessness is there
and the room empty.

It is high time to grow old. Others, younger
comport themselves with dignity, have clever points of view.
With amazement and some envy I look at them,
their confidence, their clothes, painstaking physical care
and their smiles that have been practised, like their talk.
How trim and neat they are,
well-groomed like horses, and, in the small hours,
with the wild eyes of horses. It is high time
to have oneself elected to some order and once a week
eat lunch with those of like mind and be dead.

Is there no one else at all
who rides here on the same bus
one rainy evening after bedtime
when the world seems empty?
So much shouting and yelling
remains at the station.
The further away I get
the lamps grow ever sparser
and the rain beats against the windows
that reflect the image of a stranger.
At the terminus I do not know
in what direction I must go
until someone unknown shouts: this way!
I assume that I am coming home.
And there must be quiet districts
where all the people are asleep
and only the wind seems homeless
on roads with a lot of leaves.
Faint light from some house in the distance.
It is there I am going.

The wool jams in the trouser-hook and the pocket
reaches into the lungs. A button
hangs, torn off, near the outermost finger
and the belt pulls at the throat with its ice-cold buckle.
There shoes walk on legs that are boneless
and move in time to the leather crotch;
the sleeves fall when the hands are raised with wrists
on which red scars gleam as on a dark photograph
the cars' red brake-lights between the black
carcasses of clothes. It is time to draw a knife
or sink in the mud, switch off the TV
and give oneself up to wind, clouds and night.

Tomorrow I will possess
a day without aim or meaning.
Tomorrow the skies will lift
and the wind drive mist
over the high trees.
Up towards land, into great forests,
wild game will go, clear-seeing.
If I am near sea
death will be there, it will spread
like sound on the waves.
Tomorrow, tomorrow
the coast will be steep
and unknown.

When I was younger I sought answers to questions.
Silence was an answer, if I listened
I heard the wind move, a door bang.
People came and went, I rejoiced
in the unknown, forgot it quickly,
both the joy and the surprise, at home.
Now I have begun to talk to myself
as though I wanted to know this person who talks
and listens so badly, wrapped in thought.
A few words sought their way close up to me
as though they sought protection from something
that was too difficult to see. I wrote down.
This they taught me, the words that came:
farewells are parts of everything that lives
and, when I have dreamt most strongly,
a homecoming.

I imagined that the world was outside me, great in its silence,
that that which was small, warm and bearable spoke softly,
was near. And then, this! Over the dark deeps
under the surface, deep under the water's surface those quivering deeps
    that catch stars
and, along waterways and out of the motionless choir of the reeds:
    silence.
As though a thousand screaming birds, scared flew up from the evening's
    rock
sensing that this was the world's creation, the world's destruction,
here, far in the north, in the mute, dark heart
that sees the sky's breathing like a fine mist, a wave,
heavy and great like that being space calls on with its voice's absence,
its setting sun, its darkening prayer.